MY AMERICAN STORY

GETTING OUR VOICES HEARD

HOW CAN AMERICANS CHANGE OUR SOCIETY?

Editorial Management by Oriel Square
Produced for DK by Collaborate Agency
Index by James Helling

Author Elliott Smith
Series Editor Megan DuVarney Forbes
Publisher Nick Hunter
Publisher Sarah Forbes
Publishing Project Manager Katherine Neep
Production Controller Isabell Schart
Picture Researcher Nunhoih Guite
Production Editor Shanker Prasad

First American Edition, 2023
Published in the United States by DK Publishing
1745 Broadway, 20th Floor, New York, NY 10019

A catalog record for this book
is available from the Library of Congress.
ISBN 978-0-7440-7770-4

DK books are available at special discounts when purchased
in bulk for sales promotions, premiums, fund-raising, or educational use.
For details, contact: DK Publishing Special Markets,
1745 Broadway, 20th Floor, New York, NY 10019
SpecialSales@dk.com

Printed and bound in China

The publisher would like to thank the following for their kind permission to reproduce their images:
(Key: a-above; b-below/bottom; c-center; f-far; l-left; r-right; t-top)

4 Getty Images: Hulton Archive / Staff (clb). **5 Getty Images:** Daniel Leal / AFP (cra); Paul Bersebach / MediaNews Group / Orange County Register (clb). **6 Getty Images:** Hulton Fine Art Collection / National Galleries of Scotland (clb). **9 Alamy Stock Photo:** Danvis Collection (cla); North Wind Picture Archives (bl). **10 National Portrait Gallery, Smithsonian Institution:** bequest of Charles Francis Adams; frame ccnserved with funds from the Smithsonian Women's Committee (cr). **11 Library of Congress, Washington, D.C.:** LC-DIG-ppmsca-59409/ Declaration of Independence and its signers. , ca. 1906. [United States:publisher not transcribed] Photograph. https://www.loc.gov/ item/2018757145/. (cra). **Shutterstock.com:** Everett Collection (clb). **13 Alamy Stock Photo:** Lakeview Images (cl). **Collection of the Smithsonian National Museum of African American History and Culture:** (tr). **14 Getty Images:** Archive Photos / Interim Archives (cra). **15 Library of Congress, Washington, D.C.:** LC-DIG-ppmsca-54232 / Lindsley, Harvey B., 1842-1921, photographer (cl). **16 Dreamstime. com:** Jos © Carvallido (br). **Library of Congress, Washington, D.C.:** LC-USZ62-119343/Sojourner Truth, three-quarter length portrait, standing, wearing spectacles, shawl, and peaked cap, right hand resting on cane. , 1864. [Detroit] Photograph. https://www.loc.gov/ item/97513239/. (cla); LC-DIG-ppmsca-53260/William Lloyd Garrison, abolitionist, journalist, and editor of The Liberator. , ca. 1870. Photograph. https://www.loc.gov/item/2017660623/. (bl). **18 National Portrait Gallery, Smithsonian Institution:** gift of Mrs. Alan Valentine (cla). **19 Alamy Stock Photo:** Everett Collection Historical (tl). Dreamstime.com: 3000ad (b). **20 Library of Congress, Washington, D.C.:** LC-USZ62-28195/Elizabeth Cady Stanton. , . [No Date Recorded on Caption Card] Photograph. https://www.loc.gov/item/2004670381/. (cra); Our Roll of Honor. Listing women and men who signed the Declaration of Sentiments at first Woman's Rights Convention, July 19-20. Seneca Fal s, New York, May, 1908. Manuscript/Mixed Material. https://www.loc.gov/item/rbcmiller001182/. (clb). **21 Getty Images:** Archive Photos / Chicago History Museum (tr). **Library of Congress, Washington, D.C.:** LC-DIG-ggbain-29524 / Bain News Service, publisher (cr). **22 Alamy Stock Photo:** Alpha Stock (b). **23 Library of Congress, Washington, D.C.:** LC-DIG-ggbain-39054 / Bain News Service, publisher (tr). **24 Getty Images:** Bettmann (cra). **25 Alamy Stock Photo:** The Granger Collection (br). **26 Alamy Stock Photo:** Everett Collection (b). **27 Getty Images:** The White House / Handout / Pete Souza (crb). **28 Getty Images:** Bettmann (cla). **29 Getty Images:** Bettmann (tl); Jeff Hutchens (cr). **30 Shutterstock.com:** Everett Collection (cr). **31 Alamy Stock Photo:** GRANGER - Historical Picture Archive (tl). **Getty Images:** Bettmann (br). **33 Getty Images:** Hulton Archive / Cathy Murphy (tl); Photodisc / Ariel Skelley (br). **34 Alamy Stock Photo:** Universal Images Group North America LLC / Education Images (clb). **35 Library of Congress, Washington, D.C.:** LC-USZ62-93533 / Arnold, C. D. (Charles Dudley), 1844-, photographer (br). **36 Getty Images:** Bettmann (cra, cr). **37 Shutterstock.com:** ChicagoPhotographer (cr). **38 Alamy Stock Photo:** Retro AdArchives (cla). **39 Getty Images:** Anna Moneymaker / Staff (b). **40 Library of Congress, Washington, D.C.:** LC-USZ62-133631 / United States. War Relocation Authority. (clb). **41 Getty Images:** Wally Mcnamee / Corbis (cla); Wally Skalij / Los Angeles Times (cra). **42 Getty Images:** Alastair Pike / AFP (b). **43 Alamy Stock Photo:** Molly Riley / UPI (br). **47 Alamy Stock Photo:** Everett Collection (tr). **Getty Images:** Photodisc / Ariel Skelley (br). **Shutterstock.com:** Everett Collection (cr)

All other images © Dorling Kindersley Limited

Illustrations by: Karen Saavedra

For the curious
www.dk.com

MIX
Paper | Supporting
responsible forestry
FSC™ C018179

This book was made with Forest
Stewardship Council™ certified
paper – one small step in DK's
commitment to a sustainable future.
For more information go to
www.dk.com/our-green-pledge

CONTENTS

PEOPLE POWER

★ ★

"WHEN YOU SEE SOMETHING THAT IS NOT JUST, NOT FAIR, OR NOT RIGHT, YOU HAVE TO DO SOMETHING. YOU HAVE TO SAY SOMETHING. MAKE A LITTLE NOISE." — ACTIVIST AND POLITICIAN, JOHN LEWIS

MARY MCLEOD BETHUNE WAS THE DAUGHTER OF **ENSLAVED PEOPLE.** DURING HER LIFE, SHE LED CAMPAIGNS FOR EQUALITY FOR BLACK PEOPLE AND ALL WOMEN, AND TOOK ON IMPORTANT ROLES IN GOVERNMENT.

Changes to laws are officially made by judges and are developed as part of political plans, but these changes are often driven by the passion of ordinary people. The United States is a **democratic republic**, which means that citizens have the power to choose the elected officials who will make their laws. From small, local community movements to major **campaigns** with large-scale results, people also have the power to help change society for the better.

In the 1960s, the phrase "power to the people" became popular as a wave of **grassroots** movements protested for change. However, people have made a difference in American society since the very beginning of the nation. Even today, people continue to put pressure on the government to enact laws that reflect the will of the people.

BLACK LIVES MATTER PROTESTS IN 2020 INVOLVED MILLIONS OF PEOPLE AROUND THE WORLD. THEY PROTESTED THE UNFAIR TREATMENT OF BLACK PEOPLE BY THE POLICE AND OTHER INSTITUTIONS.

SYLVIA MENDEZ —CAMPAIGNER FOR HISPANIC EDUCATION RIGHTS FROM THE AGE OF 8

DID YOU KNOW?

FOR MUCH OF AMERICAN HISTORY, **LGBTQ+** PEOPLE WERE FORCED TO KEEP THEIR PRIVATE LIVES SECRET OR FACE DISCRIMINATION. THIS STARTED TO CHANGE IN THE 1960S. HARVEY MILK WAS A LEADER OF SAN FRANCISCO'S LARGE LGBTQ+ COMMUNITY AND CHAMPIONED THEIR RIGHTS. MILK WAS MURDERED BECAUSE OF HIS CAMPAIGN. BEFORE HE DIED, HE RECORDED A POWERFUL MESSAGE URGING GAY PEOPLE TO "COME OUT, STAND UP, AND LET THE WORLD KNOW ... ONLY THAT WAY WILL WE START TO ACHIEVE OUR RIGHTS."

FIGHTING FOR
INDEPENDENCE

★ ★

In the late 1700s, the people of North America were ruled by European countries and had no say in their government. Many of the people who lived in the 13 colonies along the coast from New Hampshire to Georgia were sick of being ruled by Great Britain. They didn't like paying taxes to the British king. Many had made the dangerous journey from Europe to escape the rules of their home country.

The colonists grew angrier every time the government made them pay a new tax. The Stamp Act of 1765 taxed people on nearly every piece of paper used. The Townshend Acts of 1767 taxed just about everything else, including ... tea! But what could the colonists do? It would take several major events, started by everyday citizens, to put the colonies on their path to freedom.

BOSTON MASSACRE

Crispus Attucks was a local sailor of Black and Indigenous background. He was in Boston on March 5, 1770 when a group of angry colonists confronted a British soldier. The colonists raised such a fuss that more British soldiers were called in to calm the situation. It was later reported that someone had yelled "fire" during the fight.

Shots were fired and Attucks was one of five colonists killed that day. Attucks is often called the first casualty of the American Revolution. He was given a hero's funeral. His body was taken to Boston's Faneuil Hall, where people could view it for several days.

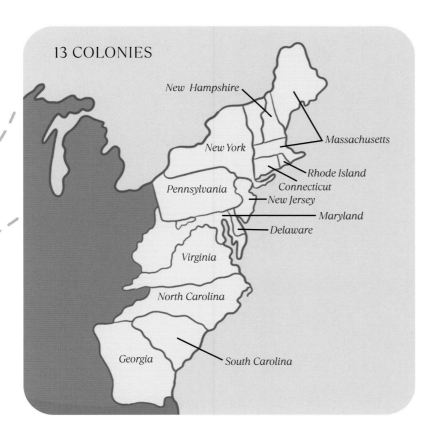

13 COLONIES

New Hampshire
Massachusetts
New York
Rhode Island
Connecticut
Pennsylvania
New Jersey
Maryland
Delaware
Virginia
North Carolina
Georgia
South Carolina

The Boston Massacre, as it would come to be known, was the first major citizen-led resistance against Great Britain. It would not be the last.

THE BOSTON TEA PARTY

★ ★

 More than three years later, colonists still felt **exploited** by British rule. The taxes and regulations by Great Britain had only grown stricter since the Boston Massacre. A mysterious group called the Sons of Liberty led the fight against the hated taxes. These merchants and tradesmen started out as regular citizens but would become key people in the birth of the U.S.

When three big tea ships arrived in Boston Harbor in December 1773, the colonists did not want to pay tax on the tea. The Massachusetts governor ordered the tax to be paid and the tea to be unloaded, but the colonists refused. Instead, the Sons of Liberty made a plan.

On the night of December 16, 1773, more than 100 colonists – many of them teenagers – boarded the three ships. In an effort to disguise themselves, they dressed as Indigenous people. They dumped almost 350 chests of tea into the water, costing about $1 million in today's money!

"We then were ordered by our commander to open the hatches and take out all the chests of tea and throw them overboard, and we immediately proceeded to execute his orders, first cutting and splitting the chests with our tomahawks, so as thoroughly to expose them to the effects of the water." – Boston Tea Party participant, George Hewes.

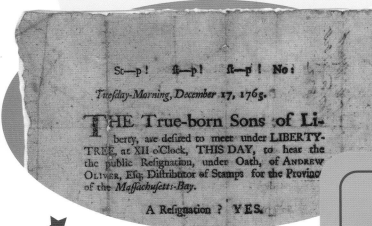

Why do you think the colonists decided to destroy this tea?

WHO WERE THE SONS OF LIBERTY?

- THEY STARTED IN BOSTON BUT THERE WERE SIMILAR GROUPS IN NEW YORK AND OTHER CITIES OR COLONIES.

- THE GROUP WAS FOUNDED TO PROTEST THE STAMP ACT AND OTHER BRITISH LAWS.

- THEY ARRANGED BOYCOTTS OF BRITISH GOODS AND ATTACKED THOSE WHO COLLECTED TAXES FOR THE BRITISH.

- SONS OF LIBERTY MEMBERS INCLUDED SAMUEL ADAMS, BENEDICT ARNOLD, PATRICK HENRY, PAUL REVERE, AND JOHN HANCOCK.

DECLARATION OF
INDEPENDENCE

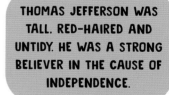

By 1775, people throughout the 13 colonies were openly revolting against the British government and King George III. A group of leaders decided to write a document that explained why they needed their own government.

WHO WERE THE FOUNDING FATHERS?

THEY WERE THE MEN WHO WORKED TO FOUND THE U.S., FROM THE DECLARATION OF INDEPENDENCE AND THE WAR THAT FOLLOWED, TO THE FOUNDING OF THE NEW NATION.

FOUNDING FATHERS INCLUDED JOHN ADAMS, SAMUEL ADAMS, BENJAMIN FRANKLIN, ALEXANDER HAMILTON, PATRICK HENRY, THOMAS JEFFERSON, JAMES MADISON, JOHN MARSHALL, GEORGE MASON, AND GEORGE WASHINGTON.

THOMAS JEFFERSON WAS TALL, RED-HAIRED AND UNTIDY. HE WAS A STRONG BELIEVER IN THE CAUSE OF INDEPENDENCE.

Thomas Jefferson took on the job of writing this document. Jefferson was a young **representative** from Virginia. It did not take him long to create the Declaration of **Independence.** Representatives of the 13 colonies approved it on July 4, 1776. As of September 1776, the colonies were officially called the United States.

The Declaration of Independence was written to inspire people in America to create a new nation. It also tried to persuade other countries to support the freedom of the colonies from Great Britain. The document listed the failures of King George III and stated that the colonies "ought to be free and independent states".

THIS CARTOON URGES THE COLONIES TO UNITE FOR INDEPENDENCE.

DID YOU KNOW?

THE **PREAMBLE** TO THE DECLARATION BECAME ITS MOST FAMOUS SECTION. THERE, JEFFERSON WROTE THAT, "WE HOLD THESE TRUTHS TO BE SELF-EVIDENT, THAT ALL MEN ARE CREATED EQUAL..."

HOWEVER, JEFFERSON COULD NOT LIVE UP TO THIS IDEAL. HE, AND MANY OF THE FOUNDING FATHERS WHO SIGNED THE DOCUMENT, ENSLAVED OTHER HUMAN BEINGS.

THE FIGHT AGAINST
SLAVERY

★ ★ ★ ★ ★ ★ ★ ★ ★ ★ ★ ★ ★ ★ ★ ★ ★ ★ ★ ★

The United States of America was formed after the war against British rule was won. However, that didn't mean everyone in the country had the same rights. While the Declaration of Independence claimed that "all men are created equal," the people of the U.S. were not treated equally at all. Slavery was a stain on the new country.

For more than 350 years, Europeans captured millions of African men, women, and children. They carried them in chains on cramped and filthy ships to the Americas. The first enslaved people in the English colony of Virginia arrived in 1619. Slavery continued to grow as the colonies officially became states. While importing enslaved people was abolished in 1808 in the U.S., it remained legal to trade people within the country. By 1860, there were more than three million enslaved people in the U.S., mainly in the southern states.

Meanwhile, people of all backgrounds fought to stop the practice. Some used religious and moral ideas. Others turned to the printed word to gain support for their cause. Some even used violence in an attempt to shock the system. As politicians were slow to act, it was the efforts of everyday citizens that helped turn public opinion against slavery.

WHO FOUGHT AGAINST SLAVERY?

- THE QUAKERS WERE THE FIRST RELIGIOUS GROUP IN BRITAIN AND AMERICA TO PROTEST SLAVERY.

- BLACK WRITERS USED PAMPHLETS, OR SMALL BOOKLETS, TO PROTEST SLAVERY IN THE NORTH.

- HARRIET BEECHER STOWE'S BOOK *UNCLE TOM'S CABIN* ANGERED SOUTHERNERS WITH ITS DEPICTIONS OF THE HORRORS OF SLAVERY.

- NAT TURNER LED A REBELLION OF ENSLAVED PEOPLE IN 1831 THAT RESULTED IN MANY DEATHS AND INCREASED TENSIONS THAT WOULD EVENTUALLY LEAD TO THE CIVIL WAR.

HARRIET TUBMAN
AND THE UNDERGROUND RAILROAD

★ ★ ★ ★ ★ ★ ★ ★ ★ ★ ★ ★ ★ ★ ★ ★ ★ ★ ★ ★

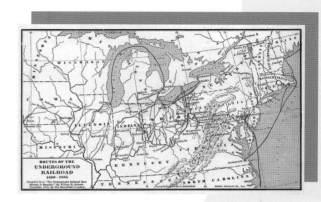

One way to fight against slavery was to help individual enslaved people. Harriet Tubman escaped from slavery herself and used her knowledge to help free others on the Underground Railroad. She traveled to plantations where enslaved people lived and helped them escape to areas where slavery was illegal. Tubman did not create the Railroad, but she was its most skilled operator. Her knowledge of the hidden trails and safe routes allowed her to free around 70 people.

Tubman never lost a passenger on her travels and was never caught. Her daring escapes inspired other anti-slavery supporters. She became known as "Moses" for her rescues. Southern slaveholders offered large rewards for her capture. Tubman supported many other anti-slavery causes, including John Brown's raid on Harpers Ferry in 1859.

WHAT WAS THE UNDERGROUND RAILROAD?

- THE RAILROAD WAS NOT ACTUALLY A RAILROAD, BUT INSTEAD A NETWORK OF PEOPLE AND PLACES DESIGNED TO HELP ENSLAVED PEOPLE ESCAPE.

- THE ROUTE STARTED IN THE SOUTH AND WENT AS FAR NORTH AS CANADA.

- HIDING PLACES ALONG THE WAY WERE CALLED STATIONS.

During the Civil War, Tubman became a spy! Dressed as an old woman, she gathered information about troop movements and supply lines. She scouted out Confederate torpedoes and helped the Union pull off daring raids.

TUBMAN'S WORK MADE HER AN ICON. HER LEGACY IS STILL RECOGNIZED TODAY.

"I had reasoned this out in my mind, there was one of two things I had a right to, liberty or death; if I could not have one, I would have the other." – Harriet Tubman

DID YOU KNOW?

TUBMAN WILL BE THE FIRST WOMAN TO APPEAR ON U.S. CURRENCY. THE $20 BILL WILL FEATURE HER IMAGE.

HEROES
OF THE ABOLITION MOVEMENT

Tubman was just one of many people who spoke out against slavery. Abolitionists wanted to abolish, or end, slavery. They took different approaches to achieve this.

★ SOJOURNER TRUTH ★

Born enslaved as Isabella Baumfree, she changed her name to Sojourner Truth after gaining her freedom in 1827. Truth's mission was to speak out against slavery. Despite not knowing how to read or write, Truth's words were powerful. Her speeches were filled with wisdom, humor, and religious stories she connected to slavery.

WILLIAM GARRISON AND ★ FREDERICK DOUGLASS ★

Garrison was a white newspaper owner. Douglass escaped slavery. The two men became linked by their abolitionist views. Garrison used his newspaper, *The Liberator,* to call for immediate freedom for all enslaved people. Douglass's autobiography about his experience with slavery became a best-seller.

★ JOHN BROWN ★

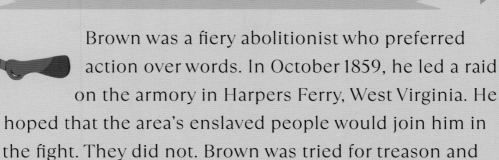

Brown was a fiery abolitionist who preferred action over words. In October 1859, he led a raid on the armory in Harpers Ferry, West Virginia. He hoped that the area's enslaved people would join him in the fight. They did not. Brown was tried for treason and hanged. His raid failed but it was one of the sparks that led to the Civil War.

IN 1865 THE THIRTEENTH AMENDMENT TO THE CONSTITUTION ABOLISHED ALL SLAVERY IN THE U.S.

★ WORDS AND ACTIONS ★

The words of **activists** like Sojourner Truth changed people's views on slavery. However, thousands of lives were lost in a terrible civil war before slavery finally ended. Do you think it was more effective for abolitionists to protest through words or actions?

WOMEN'S RIGHTS

LUCRETIA MOTT

Black Americans were not the only group who wanted change. Many people who fought slavery also wanted more rights for women. While women could not even vote in elections for the president or Congress, activists like Lucretia Mott were leading figures in campaigns like the one to abolish slavery.

Women had few rights in the U.S. They could not vote or become doctors or lawyers. Women could not go to college. Married women's lives were controlled by their husbands, and they were not allowed to own property.

Abigail Adams was the wife of the second president, John Adams. In 1776, she wrote to her husband:

"Remember the ladies, and be more generous and favorable to them than your ancestors. Do not put such unlimited power into the hands of the husbands. Remember all men would be tyrants if they could."

ABIGAIL ADAMS

Many women started to use their voices to try and change their situation. Slowly but surely, they built a network across the young country that allowed them to tackle these issues head on and make great strides toward equality. Women are still campaigning today for some rights like equal pay.

DID YOU KNOW?

THE WOMEN'S MARCH BEGAN IN 2017 TO CREATE SOCIAL CHANGE BY BRINGING TOGETHER DIVERSE COMMUNITIES OF ACTIVISTS. NEARLY 500,000 PEOPLE CAME TO WASHINGTON, D.C. TO FIGHT FOR WOMEN'S RIGHTS ACROSS A NUMBER OF ISSUES.

THE SUFFRAGE MOVEMENT

VOTES FOR WOMEN

★ ★

Elizabeth Cady Stanton was a well-educated woman from New York involved in the abolitionist movement. She was frustrated that women were left out of the political decision-making process so she created a Women's Rights Convention.

The first convention was in Seneca Falls, NY on July 19–20, 1848. There, Stanton unveiled her Declaration of Sentiments. The Declaration was based on the Declaration of Independence but included 18 reasons why women were treated unfairly.

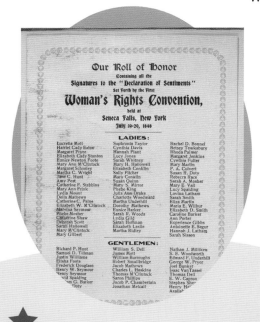

Stanton's central aim was to get women the right to vote. Teaming up with women like Susan B. Anthony and Sojourner Truth, Stanton spoke passionately about women's **suffrage**. Some male politicians and newspaper editors opposed the movement, which attracted more women to the cause.

The movement earned small victories. In 1869, the territory of Wyoming allowed women over 21 to vote. Several other western states later gave women voting rights.

There were disagreements about race, with Stanton arguing that white women should be allowed to vote before Black men. Black women like Ida B. Wells joined the cause to ensure equality for all women. The movement was mostly peaceful, however, some suffragists got themselves arrested on purpose to draw attention to the cause.

DID YOU KNOW?

IN 1925, NELLIE TAYLOE ROSS BECAME THE FIRST FEMALE GOVERNOR IN U.S. HISTORY, WINNING ELECTION IN WYOMING.

VOTING RIGHTS ★ FOR ALL ★

In 1920, the Nineteenth Amendment finally gave women the right to vote. Now women's voices could be heard. However, many state governments used literacy tests and poll taxes to prevent women of color from using their voting rights. Black, Indigenous, and other women and men of color were not fully able to vote until the 1964 Civil Rights and 1965 Voting Rights Acts.

FIGHTING WOMEN'S POVERTY

In the 1800s, many rich people thought poor people were just lazy or made bad choices in life. Poor women were often blamed for their situation. These women had few rights and could not find decent jobs.

In the early 1900s, attitudes began to change about the poor. Wealthy women could not enter politics and did not normally work paid jobs, so some decided to focus on tackling poverty. They would make a difference to society through social reform.

One way to help people was to provide safe places for them to live. Supporters set up settlement houses in poor neighborhoods to help the social welfare of the local community. In New York and Chicago, many immigrant women and their families stayed in these buildings. Jane Addams opened Hull House in Chicago in 1889. Settlement houses spread across the U.S., with more than 400 settlement houses in major cities.

HULL HOUSE BECAME A PLACE WHERE POOR WOMEN COULD RECEIVE CHILDCARE, HEALTHCARE, AND OTHER HELP.

JANE ADDAMS

For working women, pay was low and working conditions were often bad. Women had few options for better work. Josephine Shaw Lowell established the New York Consumer's League. This organization fought for better wages and conditions for women in the city. Lowell published the White List—a list of stores that treated female workers well.

CIVIL RIGHTS

★ ★ ★ ★ ★ ★ ★ ★ ★ ★ ★ ★ ★ ★ ★ ★ ★ ★ ★

Almost four million formerly enslaved people were free by the end of the Civil War. The **federal** government passed laws to help protect their rights. During the Reconstruction era (1865–1877), life improved for many African-Americans, but progress did not last. The battle for civil rights continued into modern times.

The leaders of southern states passed laws to restrict the freedom of formerly enslaved people, including laws which stopped them from voting. These laws limited the social, political, and economic freedom of African-Americans. By the 1880s, these state laws stopped Black people from living in certain neighborhoods. They stopped Black people from sharing public spaces with white people. They also made sure children of different races did not go to the same schools.

These laws lasted from the 1870s to the 1960s. They affected generations of Black families. These racist laws had a profound impact on the U.S. that continues to be felt. From home ownership and criminal justice to education, there is still a large division between the average Black person and white person because of these historical policies.

It took courageous steps by people with very little power to change not only the law, but also the way people thought about African-Americans.

WHAT ARE CIVIL RIGHTS?

- CIVIL RIGHTS ARE RIGHTS THAT ALL CITIZENS HAVE IN A DEMOCRACY.

- ALL CITIZENS SHOULD HAVE EQUAL RIGHTS, WHATEVER THEIR RACE, RELIGION, OR OTHER CHARACTERISTICS MAY BE.

- THESE RIGHTS INCLUDE THE RIGHT TO VOTE IN ELECTIONS, THE RIGHT TO EDUCATION, AND THE RIGHT TO BE TREATED FAIRLY BY POLICE AND COURTS.

ROSA PARKS
AND THE MONTGOMERY BUS BOYCOTT

★ ★ ★ ★ ★ ★ ★ ★ ★ ★ ★ ★ ★ ★ ★ ★ ★ ★ ★ ★

Racism and **segregation** were part of life in Montgomery, Alabama. For example, Black people could only sit in the back of the city bus. A driver could tell a Black person to give up their seat to a white rider if the bus was crowded.

On December 1, 1955, Rosa Parks was returning home from work. When the bus driver asked Black riders to give up their seats for a white passenger, three people got up. Parks did not, and was arrested.

ROSA PARKS BECAME KNOWN AS "THE MOTHER OF THE CIVIL RIGHTS MOVEMENT".

"People always say that I didn't give up my seat because I was tired, but that isn't true. I was not tired physically... No, the only tired I was, was tired of giving in." - Rosa Parks

Parks had spent many years working to secure rights for Black people. Her protest was the first act in a plan to **boycott** the city's buses and challenge the law. For over a year, Montgomery's Black population walked to school and work so the bus company would lose money and listen to them. They drew national attention. In 1956, the Supreme Court ruled that bus segregation was **unconstitutional**.

Parks faced abuse for her courage. As the years passed, her bravery made her an American hero. In 1999, she was awarded the Congressional Gold Medal, the highest civilian honor. When she died in 2005, Parks became the first woman to lie in honor at the U.S. Capitol.

DID YOU KNOW?

ROSA PARKS WASN'T THE FIRST TO REFUSE TO GIVE UP HER SEAT. NINE MONTHS BEFORE PARKS, 15 YEAR OLD CLAUDETTE COLVIN DID THE SAME THING IN BIRMINGHAM, ALABAMA. HER STORY IS OFTEN OVERLOOKED.

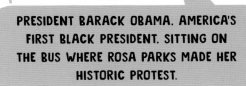

PRESIDENT BARACK OBAMA, AMERICA'S FIRST BLACK PRESIDENT, SITTING ON THE BUS WHERE ROSA PARKS MADE HER HISTORIC PROTEST.

MARTIN LUTHER KING, JR.

The Civil Rights movement had many heroes. However, no one symbolizes the way people can change society more than Martin Luther King, Jr.

King was a young minister working in Alabama when he became a leader during the Montgomery bus boycott. During that time, King faced abuse and had his home bombed. The success of the boycott showed that King's methods could work.

He was elected president of the Southern Christian Leadership Conference in 1957. King became the face of the campaign for civil rights, using non-violent techniques to promote racial equality. When people across the country saw peaceful protests and marches met with violence from the authorities, the movement won more support.

BLACK LIVES MATTER

BLM

King was arrested more than 20 times and his life was under constant threat. Still, he fought tirelessly for equality. In 1963, more than 250,000 people joined the March on Washington for a peaceful protest. King's "I Have a Dream" speech given that day remains one of the great spoken works in world history.

With King's leadership and the hard work of dozens of other civil rights leaders, the campaign forced changes to the law. The Civil Rights Act of 1957 protected voting rights. The Civil Rights Act of 1964 guaranteed equal employment for all. The Fair Housing Act of 1968 stopped discrimination in housing based on race, sex, or religion.

POLITICIAN AND CIVIL RIGHTS ACTIVIST JOHN LEWIS

★KING'S LEGACY★

King was murdered on April 4, 1968 in Memphis. But his legacy in the Civil Rights movement, and to the U.S., will never be forgotten. His methods of peaceful protest have been adopted by activists around the world. The Black Lives Matter movement is an example of how people can protest without violence.

CHANGING
WORKERS' LIVES

★ ★ ★ ★ ★ ★ ★ ★ ★ ★ ★ ★ ★ ★ ★ ★ ★ ★ ★

We all need to work to pay our bills, but workers have not always been paid fairly. As American labor moved from small craftspeople working independently to large-scale production in factories, workers needed protection through regulations. Many workers also organized themselves into trade unions.

WHAT IS A TRADE UNION?

- A TRADE UNION OR LABOR UNION IS AN ORGANIZATION OF WORKERS IN A PROFESSION OR COMPANY.

- MEMBERS OF THE TRADE UNION WORK TOGETHER TO AGREE ON PAY AND CONDITIONS WITH EMPLOYERS, AND ENSURE ALL WORKERS ARE TREATED FAIRLY.

- TRADE UNIONS CAN ORGANIZE PROTESTS OR STOP WORK IN A STRIKE TO PROTECT WORKERS' RIGHTS.

DID YOU KNOW?

THE FIRST RECORDED STRIKE IN AMERICAN HISTORY OCCURRED IN 1768, WHEN TAILORS IN NEW YORK FOUGHT BACK AGAINST WAGE REDUCTIONS.

Samuel Gompers was one of the earliest voices to speak on behalf of workers. Gompers helped found the American Federation of Labor (AFL), which united trade unions. Gompers's goal for the AFL's members was simple. He wanted, "more wages, more leisure, more liberty" for everyone by using collective action.

Mother Jones was another early labor movement activist. She helped mine workers who were striking in the early 1900s and convinced them to join unions. She also pushed to end the practice of child labor, which was common at the time.

Unions were not safe from racism. Many Black workers had very little protection and were forced to work extra hours. A. Philip Randolph was a groundbreaking Black labor organizer. His work with train porters led to the formation of the Brotherhood of Sleeping Car Porters, the first Black-led union to join the AFL.

CESAR CHAVEZ
AND
DOLORES HUERTA

★ ★ ★ ★ ★ ★ ★ ★ ★ ★ ★ ★ ★ ★ ★ ★ ★ ★ ★

Millions of immigrants worked to build the Western lands of the U.S. First, there were Chinese, Filipino, and Japanese workers. By the 1940s, most farm workers were Mexican **migrants**. These workers were underpaid and often lived in poor conditions. Farm owners squashed any plans to organize trade unions.

Cesar Chavez was one of those workers. He dropped out of school in the eighth grade and started working to support his family. He had first-hand knowledge of hard work and low pay. In 1962, Chavez formed the National Farm Workers Association. Chavez found a partner in Dolores Huerta, a former schoolteacher. Huerta believed the best way to help people was through community organization.

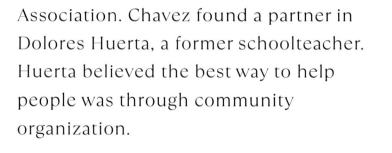

In 1965, Chavez and Huerta formed the United Farm Workers Union (UFW). A few months later, the UFW launched its biggest protest, the Delano Grape Strike. This was a five-year campaign that featured walkouts, marches, and boycotts. Chavez went on a 25-day hunger strike, refusing to eat as an example of the non-violent tactics the union would use in its fight. In 1970, the grape producers finally did the right thing. They signed their contracts with the union, which provided better pay, benefits, and protections for migrant workers.

Chavez and Huerta continued to advocate for farm workers over the next several decades, improving pay and safety measures.

DID YOU KNOW?

THE DELANO GRAPE STRIKE DREW NATIONAL ATTENTION, WITH CIVIL RIGHTS LEADERS LIKE MARTIN LUTHER KING JR. REACHING OUT TO THE UFW TO OFFER SUPPORT.

RIGHTS FOR INDIGENOUS PEOPLE

★ ★

There were millions of **Indigenous** people living throughout the Americas when the first settlers arrived from Europe. Settlers tried a variety of tactics to gain land from the Indigenous peoples. While some deals were made between the colonists and Indigenous nations, the colonists took lots of Indigenous peoples' land by force or **deception**.

DID YOU KNOW?

COLONISTS BROUGHT DISEASES LIKE SMALLPOX, INFLUENZA, AND MEASLES. THESE WERE NEW TO THE INDIGENOUS PEOPLE, WHO HAD NO NATURAL PROTECTION AGAINST THEM. THIS WEAKENED INDIGENOUS NATIONS AND MADE IT EASY FOR COLONISTS TO TAKE CONTROL OF THEIR LAND.

The **oppression** of Indigenous people is another dark element in American history. Their land was forcibly taken and their economic power reduced. Treaties that Indigenous peoples signed with the U.S. government were often ignored. Frequent wars between Indigenous people and the U.S. government led to further loss of life and land for Indigenous nations. Events like the Trail of Tears forced more than 60,000 Indigenous people off their land in the 1800s. The conflict continued into the early 1900s.

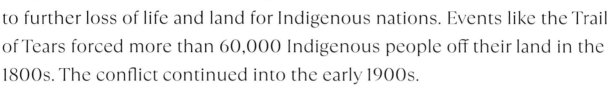

USING THE SUPREME COURT

The 20th century saw a rise in Indigenous protests. Janet McCloud was a member of the Tulalip Tribes in the northwestern part of the U.S. who fought for the right for her people to catch fish in Washington. The case went all the way to the Supreme Court. In 1974, the court ruled that the tribes were entitled to half the salmon and steelhead catch in Washington.

"They made us many promises, more than I can remember, but they kept but one: they promised to take our land and they took it." - Red Cloud, a leader of the Lakota people during the Indian Wars

INDIGENOUS MOVEMENTS
FOR CHANGE

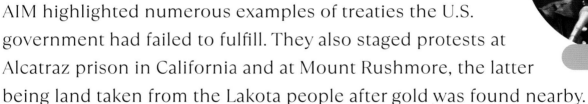

AMERICAN INDIAN MOVEMENT

DENNIS BANKS

In 1968, Dennis Banks and Russell Means formed an organization named the American Indian Movement (AIM). The organization was started to fight poverty and discrimination against Indigenous people who had moved into cities. Soon, they expanded their focus to deal with wider issues.

RUSSELL MEANS

AIM highlighted numerous examples of treaties the U.S. government had failed to fulfill. They also staged protests at Alcatraz prison in California and at Mount Rushmore, the latter being land taken from the Lakota people after gold was found nearby.

In 1973, more than 200 Indigenous people occupied Wounded Knee, the site where the Sioux nation was massacred in 1890 by U.S. troops. AIM held 11 residents hostage for 71 days, clashing with federal agents. AIM wanted the U.S. government to respect the treaties made with tribes. Wounded Knee put the problems of Indigenous people on the world stage for the first time.

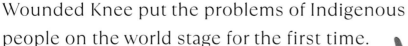

Eventually, AIM surrendered and its leaders were arrested. Other movements took its place to seek equality for Indigenous people. Today, activists like Nathan Phillips and Madonna Thunder Hawk have led the fight against the construction of oil pipelines on Indigenous nations' lands in North Dakota.

INDIGENOUS IMAGES

INDIGENOUS ORGANIZATIONS HAVE ARGUED THAT SPORTS TEAMS SHOULD NOT USE NICKNAMES OR IMAGERY THAT EXPLOITS THEIR CULTURE. RECENTLY THE WASHINGTON NFL TEAM AND THE CLEVELAND BASEBALL TEAM CHANGED THEIR NAMES TO ELIMINATE INDIGENOUS IMAGERY.

CLEVELAND'S MAJOR LEAGUE BASEBALL TEAM WAS KNOWN AS THE INDIANS. IN 2021, THEY OFFICIALLY CHANGED THE CLUB'S NAME TO THE GUARDIANS.

★ RIGHTS FOR HAWAIIANS ★

The U.S. first took control of Hawaii in 1898 and it became a state in 1950. When the U.S. government took over, they made no agreement with indigenous Hawaiians. Since the 1980s, many indigenous Hawaiians have campaigned for more rights over their land. Some indigenous Hawaiian people argue that Hawaii should be independent.

REPARATIONS

★ ★ ★ ★ ★ ★ ★ ★ ★ ★ ★ ★ ★ ★ ★ ★ ★ ★ ★ ★

Many activists have argued that reparations should be paid to groups that have suffered injustice in the past. Reparations are money paid to a particular group that has been seriously wronged. Activists argue that groups such as Black Americans and Indigenous people still have fewer opportunities because of their history. Reparations woulds not excuse the behavior, nor would it fix the larger problems, but it would acknowledge that wrongs were done in the past.

Indigenous nations have received money and land to recognize that they were forced to leave their land by the U.S. government for a very long time.

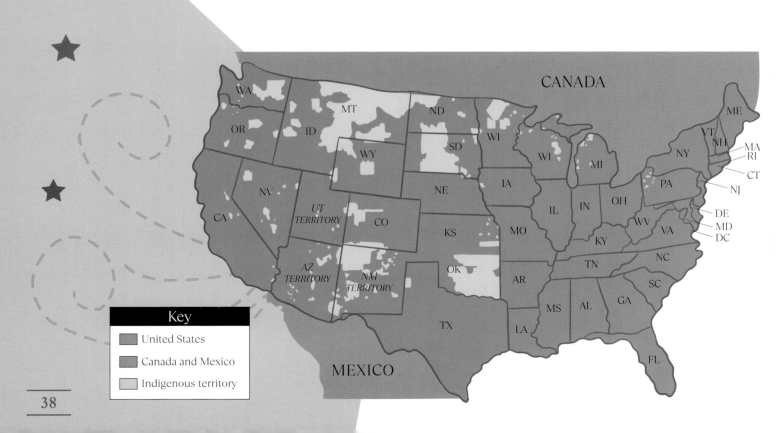

Key	
▓	United States
▓	Canada and Mexico
░	Indigenous territory

★ REPARATIONS FOR SLAVERY ★

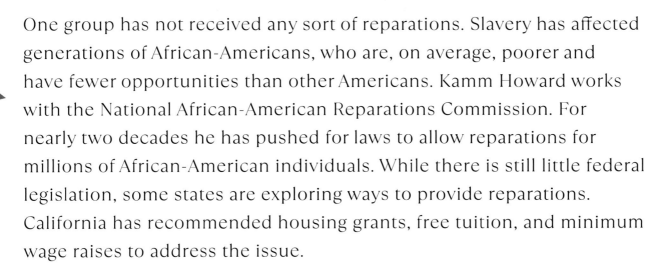

One group has not received any sort of reparations. Slavery has affected generations of African-Americans, who are, on average, poorer and have fewer opportunities than other Americans. Kamm Howard works with the National African-American Reparations Commission. For nearly two decades he has pushed for laws to allow reparations for millions of African-American individuals. While there is still little federal legislation, some states are exploring ways to provide reparations. California has recommended housing grants, free tuition, and minimum wage raises to address the issue.

In 2021, Evanston, Illinois became the first city to make reparations to Black residents. The city plans to give $10 million to Black residents to make up for what it calls "historical harm". While the plan has its critics, some people say it's a promising first step towards justice.

THE HARM IS IN OUR GENES

JAPANESE
INTERNMENT

An example of a successful campaign for reparations led by ordinary people, was the campaign against the way the U.S. treated Japanese-Americans during World War II, when the U.S. was at war with Japan.

After the Japanese attacked Pearl Harbor in 1941, panic set in across the country. In reaction to the fear, President Franklin D. Roosevelt signed a law on February 19, 1942 allowing U.S. military forces to remove Japanese people from areas they set as military zones. The order applied to all Japanese people, whether they were Issei, first-generation immigrants to the U.S., or American citizens born in the U.S. but with Japanese parents. It essentially removed constitutional rights of Japanese-Americans and painted them as enemies of the U.S.

Tens of thousands of Japanese-Americans were forced to live in **internment** camps. These internment camps were also known as American concentration camps, relocation centers, or detention centers. After the war ended, many Japanese-Americans struggled to re-adjust to normal life after they had been treated as enemies.

JUSTICE FOR JAPANESE-AMERICANS

John Tateishi was one of these Japanese-Americans. He was around three when his family was sent to an internment camp. The memories never left him. In 1975, Tateishi became involved with the redress program of the Japanese American Citizens League (JACL), the nation's oldest and largest Asian-American civil rights organization.

Tateishi and many others fought for more than a decade to educate and inform people about Japanese internment. Their efforts resulted in the Civil Liberties Act of 1988. This law gave surviving Japanese-Americans $20,000 in reparations and a formal apology from President Ronald Reagan for their imprisonment during World War II.

ENVIRONMENTAL
CHANGE

★ ★ ★ ★ ★ ★ ★ ★ ★ ★ ★ ★ ★ ★ ★ ★ ★ ★ ★

While some battles for change have been won, activists are still trying to highlight important issues. Environmental activists, such as Rachel Carson and Ralph Nader, have worked for decades to educate the population about the dangers of harmful chemicals and the risks of climate change caused by human activities. The eco-movement now features many young activists on the front lines for change.

★YOUNG ACTIVISTS★

In 2018, teenager Jamie Margolin co-founded Zero Hour. This youth-led climate organization had a major boost in publicity when it sued the state of Washington over the effects of wildfires. Zero Hour led dozens of youth climate marches and Margolin testified before Congress alongside Swedish activist Greta Thunberg.

MS. THUNBERG   MS. MARGOLIN

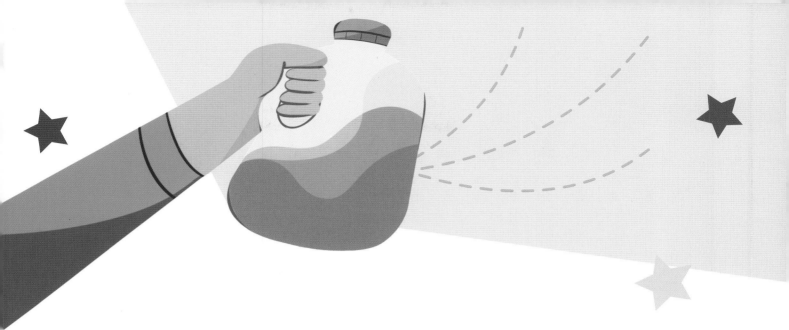

In Flint, Michigan, corporate and city mismanagement resulted in water that contained lead and made people sick. Many people protested during the Flint water crisis. One of those people was a young girl named Mari Copeny, who became a hero for her efforts to get clean drinking water.

Copeny became known as "Little Miss Flint" after she wrote a letter to President Obama when she was 8 years old. She wanted the president to meet her in Flint. Obama wrote back to Mari and would sign legislation to help Flint's problems. But Copeny wasn't finished with her work. She continued to hand out thousands of water bottles and work as a Women's March Ambassador.

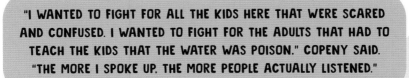

"I WANTED TO FIGHT FOR ALL THE KIDS HERE THAT WERE SCARED AND CONFUSED. I WANTED TO FIGHT FOR THE ADULTS THAT HAD TO TEACH THE KIDS THAT THE WATER WAS POISON." COPENY SAID. "THE MORE I SPOKE UP, THE MORE PEOPLE ACTUALLY LISTENED."

IT'S YOUR TURN

Reading about the efforts of everyday people who helped change society, you may be wondering: how can I campaign for change? There are many ways to start making a difference, and not one of them is too small.

★ VOLUNTEER ★

Take some time to help others. Working at a local shelter or helping pack lunches for those in need is a great way to make an impact on your community.

★ DONATE ★

Collect loose change in a jar at your house or at school and then find a local charity that you can donate the money to.

★ START A PROJECT ★

Is there an issue in society that you're passionate about? You can create your own fundraising campaign to help raise money for your cause. Or, you can educate people on the issue with a table at your local farmer's market.

★ WRITE A LETTER ★

Find out who your local and/or state representatives are. Write them a letter explaining your position on a particular issue and ask them to consider passing legislation to help.

CREATE A POSTER

Find a topic you want people to learn more about and create an informative poster about it. Let them know how they can get involved to help your cause.

★ USE SOCIAL MEDIA ★

Word travels fast on social media. Using blogs, memes, and images can help spread information quickly. Social media can therefore inform large audiences about a problem and offer potential solutions.

Don't be afraid to speak out or take action if you want to make a change. You'll likely find support from family and friends!

GLOSSARY

abolition
putting an end to something, for example the abolition of slavery

activist
someone who campaigns for change in a particular area of society

amendment
change or addition to a legal document, such as a constitution

boycott
to refuse to use or buy something as a type of protest

campaign
protest or argue for change

citizen
a member of a country, either because they were born there or have chosen it as their home

civil rights
rights to equal treatment and protection by the law, such as in the right to vote

colony
place that is ruled by another country

deception
lying or doing something to trick someone

democracy
political system in which the government is chosen by citizens voting in an election

enslaved person
person who is forced to work without payment and is treated as property, without the rights that other people have

equality
situation where all people are treated fairly and have equal opportunities

federal
the name for the U.S. national government or any government with powers shared between states and a national government

grassroots
relating to or coming from ordinary people

independence
ability to be in control of oneself, such as by setting up a new government

indigenous
original people who lived in a particular area

internment
imprisonment

legacy
the long-lasting impact of a person or event

LGBTQ+
abbreviation including the initial letters of lesbian, gay, bisexual, transgender and queer, which are used to describe a person's sexual orientation or gender identity

migrant
someone who moves from one place to another to live, such as for work or to avoid conflict

oppress
persecute or treat a group of people unfairly

preamble
introduction or first part of a document

reparations
money or other benefit given to make amends for a wrong

representative
someone who is chosen to represent a group of people, such as an elected member of Congress

segregation
the separation of people based on race or another characteristic

suffrage
the right to vote in elections

unconstitutional
not allowed according to the rules in a constitution

INDEX

★ ★